OBJECT TALKS

FOR SPECIAL OCCASIONS

by
Verna L. Kokmeyer

Standard®
PUBLISHING

Cincinnati, Ohio

TO FRANK
for his encouragement and example of joyful sharing

Cover design by Diana Walters
Inside design by Dina Sorn

All Scripture quotations, unless otherwise indicated, are taken from the *International Children's Bible®, New Century Version®,* copyright © 1986, 1988 by Tommy Nelson™, a division of Thomas Nelson, Inc., Nashville, Tennessee 37214. Used by permission.

Scripture quotations marked (*TLB*) are taken from *The Living Bible,* copyright © 1971. Used by permission of Tyndale House Publishers, Carol Stream, Illinois 60188. All rights reserved.

Published by Standard Publishing, Cincinnati, Ohio
www.standardpub.com

ISBN-13: 978-0-7847-1269-6
ISBN-10: 0-7847-1269-7

17 16 15 14 13 12   10 11 12 13 14 15 16 17 18

Occasion/Scripture	Theme	Objects	Page
New Year *Ephesians 5:15, 16*	Choose wisely	New silver coin	5
Children's Day *Corinthians 15:57*	Children's rewards	Trophy/medal	6
Valentine's Day *Isaiah 43:1*	We belong to Jesus	Valentines	7
Palm Sunday *Psalm 34:1*	Unending praise	Palm branches	8
Easter *Hebrews 10:12, 14*	Sin destroys	Lilies, scissors	9
Easter *1 Corinthians 6:20*	Jesus paid for our sins	Price tags	10
Mother's Day *Thessalonians 2:7, 8*	Mothers are special	Jewelry box	11
Memorial Day *Psalm 77:11, 12*	Remembering others	Picture	12
Father's Day *John 20:17*	A gift for father	Two gifts	13
Fourth of July *Psalm 119:44, 45*	Freedom in Christ	Sparkler, matches	14
Labor Day *Colossians 1:29*	God's power within us	Bubble gum	15
Thanksgiving *Psalm 30:11*	Giving thanks	Kitten	16
Thanksgiving *Psalm 100:4*	Come with thanks	"No Trespassing" sign	17
Advent *Matthew 3:2, 3*	Preparing for Jesus	Computer disc	18
Christmas *Romans 12:1*	Salvation	Mirror	19
Christmas *2 Corinthians 9:15*	Accept God's gift	Wrapped candy canes	20
Christmas *Luke 2:11*	Christmas is Jesus	Curling ribbon	21
Year End *2 Corinthians 4:16*	Filled with God's power	Balloons	22
Baptism *2 Corinthians 1:22*	Belonging to God	Wax and Seal	23
Baptism *2 Corinthians 5:17*	A new creation	White cardboard, blue & yellow markers	24
Bible Study *Psalm 119:9*	God's Word	Thermos	25

Commission *Hebrews 13:20*	Equipping for service	Helium balloons, and bricks	26
Evangelism *Romans 12:10, 13*	Putting others first	Straws	27
Missions *Galatians 5:13, 14*	Serving others	Crackers	28
Visitors *Romans 15:7*	Warm welcome	Clothes	29
Spring *Psalm 136:1*	God's love	Daisies	30
Spring *Psalm 76:1, 5*	God's protection	Turtle	31
Spring *Psalm 139:7, 9-12*	God is everywhere	Pussy willow	32
Summer *Proverbs 16:18*	Pride	Marshmallows	33
Summer *Ephesians 2:9, 10*	Salvation is a gift	Sticks	34
Summer *Romans 15:5*	Unity; working together	S'mores, heat source	35
Summer *Psalm 147:1*	Praise	Hamb/Hdog with buns	36
Summer *Psalm 32:10*	God's love	Life jacket	37
Summer *James 2:24, 26*	Faith without works	Water toboggan	38
Summer *John 4:23, 24*	Worship from the heart	Ice cream cone	39
Summer *1 Thessalonians 5:21, 22*	Avoid temptation	Fishing lures	40
Summer *John 3:16*	Eternal life	Fly swatter	41
Summer *Philippians 2:1, 2*	Unity	Water skis, tow rope	42
Autumn *1 John 1:9*	Forgiven sin	No. 2 pencil	43
Autumn *Luke 6:45*	Filled with good things	Backpack	44
Autumn *Romans 12:6*	All have talents	Colored leaves	45
Winter *Colossians 3:13, 14*	Forgiving each other	Downhill skis and boots	46
Winter *Philippians 2:4, 5*	Fellowship	Mitten, glove	47
Winter *Hebrews 13:8*	Jesus never changes	Cassette, snowballs	48

CHOOSE WISELY

THEME: Make wise choices on how to "spend" the new year.

OBJECT: New silver coin

TEXT: Be very careful how you live. Do not live like those who are not wise. Live wisely. I mean that you should use every chance you have for doing good. *Ephesians 5: 15, 16*

APPLICATION:

Can anyone tell me what the date is today? *(Responses.)* Yes, today is January ___, 20__. *(Fill in correct dates.)* We're starting a brand new year! Happy New Year! To help us think about this new year, I brought along a new silver coin. See how clean and shiny it is? Every year, new silver coins are made with a new date on them. The new date makes them different from all of the older silver coins.

What are some ways in which I can use this silver coin? *(Responses.)* I can put it in my pocket, and if there are no holes in my pocket, it will stay safe. What do you think of that idea? *(Responses.)* I could sit and look at it every day. *(Hold it close to your eye, and far away. Shine it on your shirt, and put it back in your pocket.)* Would that be a good use for my new silver coin? *(No.)*

Wait—I have another idea! Let's play with it! *(Hold it in your eye as you would an eyeglass. Then toss it up in the air a few times and catch it.)* Is this a good way to use my money? *(No.)*

I know! *(Smile.)* Let's spend it! *(Frown.)* But if I buy something with it, I'd probably never see the same silver coin again. This is not an easy decision, is it?

Just as we have to carefully plan how to use money, we must plan carefully how to use the new year God has given us. Just as this silver coin has a new date on it, our new year has brand new days in it—and those days will be different from all the days before. And the best part is that we don't have to make the same mistakes as before! Each new day brings a fresh new start!

Suppose we decide to sit in the same place every day and just watch the new year go by—or maybe just play all year. Would either of these be the best use of all of our time? *(No.)* Why not? *(Responses.)* It's not bad to have fun, but there are other things we need to do if we are going to use our days wisely. What are some ways we can do this? *(Responses.)* Once we've used our time, we will never have the same hours to use again, so we must try to choose wisely—and that's not always easy.

Earlier, I asked *you* to help me decide what to do with this silver coin. Now, who do you think can help us choose what to do with the time in our brand new year? *(God.)* What are some ways God would want us to spend our time? *(Discuss: Help others without griping; grow, not only in size, but also in how much we know about God; make Jesus a special friend by spending time talking with him.)*

This is a brand new year—don't waste a second of it! Let's ask God to help us use our time wisely in 20__.

PRAYER:

God, you've given us a new year. Help us to spend our time wisely in ways that are pleasing to you. Amen.

CHILDREN'S DAY
THE WINNER iS YOU

THEME: God gives rewards to children.

OBJECTS: Trophies, awards and/or medals

TEXT: "But we thank God! He gives us the victory through our Lord Jesus Christ."   *1 Corinthians 15:57*

APPLiCATiON:

Wait until you see what I have with me today! People get really excited when they get anything like this. *(Show trophy.)* You or someone you know may have a bowling trophy, a baseball plaque, or a certificate for never missing a day of school. Some kids get ribbons for animals they've raised, or races they've run. What kind of people get prizes? *(Winners.)* Awards go to people who do something special.

Do people get trophies for being kind? *(No.)* Do kids get awards for being good, for picking up toys or helping others? *(Not usually.)* Do you think anyone notices? *(Maybe.)* I've got great news for you. The Bible tells us that God doesn't miss a thing. Nothing we do goes unnoticed. He's watching us right now. *(Illustrate by giving an example of something he just saw happen as the children joined you.)* God knows when you are kind, patient, or go out of your way to help others. He even helps us do good things, and rewards those who serve him.

Today is Children's Sunday. We are all proud of each of you. We have watched you grow big and strong. Many times we have seen you help others. Who else has seen you? *(God.)* God gives eternal life as a reward to all who accept Jesus as their Savior and behave in a way that is pleasing to God. Perhaps the good things you do don't earn awards, but you are a winner in God's eyes, and he has a trophy for you!

PRAYER:

Lord, thank you for knowing the things we do to serve you. Thank you for blessing us here on earth, and for the blessing you have prepared for us in Heaven. Amen.

VALENTINE'S DAY
BE HIS

THEME: We belong to Jesus.

OBJECTS: Valentine's Day cards (can be handmade). One reads "Be Mine." Smaller valentines with "Be His" and the verse below could be given to children.

TEXT: Now this is what the Lord says . . . "Don't be afraid, because I have saved you. I have called you by name, and you are mine." *Isaiah 43:1*

APPLICATION:

Have you given out any valentines? I brought some with me today. Let's look at them. *(Share the cards, ending with one that reads "Be Mine.")* I wanted to give out lots of cards that say "Be Mine" to some special people who I want to be my close friends. My valentine reads "Be Mine," but will my friends ever really belong to me? *(No.)* Still, there is someone I do belong to. Our Bible verse reminds me that I belong to Jesus, and that I can invite my friends to belong to him too. So let's change this valentine, OK? I'm going to scratch out the "mine," and write in "his." *("Be His" can be written on the other side of the card also.)* We belong to Jesus because he gave his life for us by dying on the cross for our sins. Can you imagine having a Valentine who loves us so much that he actually gave his own life for us? Jesus invites us, not only on Valentine's Day, but every day, to choose to belong to him.

PRAYER:

Thank you, God, for sending Jesus to pay the price so that we can belong to you. Amen.

PRAISE HiM!

THEME: Unending praise

OBJECTS: Enough palm branches for each child to have one (can be artificial)

TEXT: I will praise the Lord no matter what happens. I will constantly speak of his glories and grace.
Psalm 34:1, TLB

APPLiCATiON:

What are some events that we go to where we get really excited? *(Sports events, plays, recitals, holiday parades, etc.)* And when we are really excited, what do we do? *(Cheer, shout, clap, wave our arms, etc.)*

Today is "Palm Sunday." Does anyone know why we call this day, "Palm Sunday?" *(Responses.)* This palm branch *(show)* reminds us of an exciting event that happened to Jesus just before he was killed. Jesus was coming into the town of Jerusalem, riding a donkey, and many people had heard about him and all the miracles he had done. They believed he really was the Son of God, and they were very excited to see him. They began to show their excitement in just the same way we do when we are full of energy and enthusiasm at a special event! They shouted and cheered and waved—but they not only waved their arms, they also waved branches like this one and shouted, "Hosanna," just as we shout to cheer our favorite sports team. "Hosanna" means "save now."

While it is a lot of fun to clap and shout at a special event, it's even more important to clap and praise Jesus for who he is and for everything he's done for us. We don't usually wave branches when we praise Jesus, but I think it would be great for us to do it today, since it's "Palm Sunday." Let's wave our branches and praise him together just like the people of Jerusalem did. *(Lead children in waving their branches and saying, "Hosanna, blessed is he who comes in the name of the Lord!" a few times.)*

What are some other ways in which we can praise Jesus? *(Discuss singing, praying and reading his Word.)* When we stop and think about how much Jesus loves us and all he has given us, who wouldn't want to praise him? Let's try to praise God every day, not just in church on Sunday. You can praise him in your room or even while you're doing your chores around the house. In Jerusalem people recognized who Jesus was and praised him excitedly and without hesitation. Let's praise him today, and go on to praise him tomorrow, the next day, and every day.

PRAYER:

Lord, we love you, and will praise you each and every day of our lives. Amen.

EASTER

WHOLE AGAIN

THEME: Sin destroys but Jesus restores.

OBJECTS: Two Easter lilies, scissors

TEXT: But Christ offered one sacrifice for sins, and it is good forever. . . . With one sacrifice he made perfect forever those who are being made holy. *Hebrews 10:12, 14*

APPLICATION:

Today is Easter Sunday. What special event do we celebrate at Easter? *(Discuss the resurrection of Jesus.)* I brought along some beautiful lillies to help us talk about this special day. Whenever I see a lily, I think of Easter, and what it means to me. When God first created people, he made them perfect—just like this beautiful lily. But they didn't stay that way for long. Why not? *(Responses.)* People began sinning and that sin began to destroy, little by little. What are some ways in which we sin? *(Responses.)* Maybe we lie—not a big lie, just a little one. *(Cut a bit off the lily.)* We promise we'll do something, but we don't really plan to do it *(cut)*, or we don't make the time to keep the promise. Sometimes we hurt people and say mean things *(cut)*, or take something that doesn't belong to us. *(Cut off pieces until the entire lily is destroyed.)* What happened here? My lily is no longer the perfect flower it once was. When we sin, we are no longer the way God created us. That's the bad news.

The good news is that when Jesus died in our place, he made it possible for us to be forgiven of the wrong things we do, and become perfect in God's sight once again. *(Take out the other lily.)* And that's why we celebrate Easter. By dying for our sins, Jesus gave us a chance to become whole again!

Just as I put this beautiful lily in place of the old, damaged one, Jesus has changed our lives. He took away the sin that destroyed us, and when we ask him into our lives, he puts us back together and makes us whole again.

Jesus, thank you for giving your life for us and taking away our sin. Thank you for making us whole and perfect in God's sight! Amen.

EASTER
THE HiGH COST

THEME: Jesus paid for our sins with his life.

OBJECTS: Three items ranging in value with price tags attached; a hidden price tag on yourself

TEXT: You were bought by God for a price. So honor God with your bodies.

1 Corinthians 6:20

APPLiCATiON:

How many of you like to go shopping? I brought along some things you might buy, complete with price tags. We are going to play a game. Let's put these things in a line, starting with the item that costs the least, right up to the one that is the most expensive. *(Move the products around until most agree that they are in the correct order.)*

Oh, how could I forget? Something else has a price tag on it. *(Discover a price tag in your sleeve.)* Me! Where do I fit in? What am I worth compared to these other items? *(Responses.)* I suppose my life is more valuable than *(name the other objects)*, so let's put me here at the end as what costs the most, OK?

Now, let's take a look at all the prices. *(After checking the value of the other items, discover the price on yourself—the word "Jesus" is on the price tag.)*

The Bible tells us, "You were bought by God for a price" (1 Corinthians 6:20). That price was more than ever has been paid for anything else in the world. The price was the life of Jesus. Jesus died for our sins so that we can have eternal life.

PRAYER:

Thank you, God, for Jesus, who died for our sins so that we can live forever. Amen.

MoM CARES

THEME: Mothers share their love.

OBJECT: A jewelry box

TEXT: "We were very gentle with you. We were like a mother caring for her little children. Because we loved you, we were happy to share God's Good News with you." *1 Thessalonians 2:7, 8*

APPLICATION:

Check out this box. *(Hold up a jewelry box.)* What could it be used for? *(Discuss/to hold jewelry.)* Jewelry boxes come in different sizes, shapes and colors. Some people even have locks on their jewelry boxes. Why would someone put a lock on a box? *(To protect what's inside because it is valuable.)* The most special part of a jewelry box is what it holds inside. Who cares what the box looks like on the outside?

Today is Mother's Day. Like jewelry boxes, mothers don't all look alike. Some are short and others are tall. While some are thin, many share my love for chocolate cake *(pat your tummy, if appropriate)*. A mother may have black hair, red hair, or even blond hair. It doesn't matter what your mom looks like. It is the love inside her that is important. A mother's love is so special that when gentleness is described in the Bible it is compared to a "mother caring for her little children."

How do moms show their love for us? *(Discuss, including her telling us about Jesus.)* Moms tell us about Jesus, but they also put Band-Aids on our scraped knees and give us hugs when we feel bad.

Mother's Day is an important day because moms are very special. Don't forget to wish your mom a Happy Mother's Day and when you do, be sure to thank her for sharing the faith, love, and kindness she has inside.

PRAYER:

Lord, our moms are all different, but we thank you for the special love they have for each of us. Amen.

TiME To REMEMBER

THEME: Remember what others have done for us.

OBJECTS: Picture of someone who has done much for you in the past

TEXT: I remember what the Lord did. I remember the miracles you did long ago. I think about all the things you did. I think about what you have done. *Psalm 77:11, 12*

APPLiCATioN:

This picture is of someone who has done many things for me. It is a picture of my mother. *(Use whomever you wish.)* When I see this picture, I remember all the times she cooked food for me and kept my clothes clean. Most important of all, she taught me about Jesus, and how to love him. Although my mom is in Heaven now, my life is different because of all she did for me in the past.

On Memorial Day we remember special people who are no longer living. We think about all they have done for us. Some are friends or loved ones. We also remember soldiers who have given their lives for our country. As we remember them today, on this Memorial Day weekend, let's also remember our special God who has done so much for us, and who keeps doing things for us each day. Can you think of some things he does for us? *(List.)* Memorial Day is a time to remember people who have done a lot for us. Let's think about those special people. And then, let's especially remember—and give thanks to—God, who continues to give us so much every day.

PRAYER:

Lord, we remember all you've done for us, and we give you thanks. Amen.

FOR FATHERS WHO WANT EVERYTHING

THEME: We have two fathers.

OBJECTS: Two gift-wrapped packages

TEXT: "Jesus said to her, 'Don't hold me. I have not yet gone up to the Father. But go to my brothers and tell them this: "I am going back to my Father and your Father. I am going back to my God and your God."'"
John 20:17

APPLICATION:

Are any of you planning to give your dad a gift for Father's Day? I don't want you to give away any secrets, but what kinds of things make great Father's Day gifts? *(Share ideas.)* Some of the dads I've talked to need socks and ties; others would like more fishing gear. When I shopped for my gifts, I realized I needed two Father's Day gifts. *(Hold up packages.)* Why would I need two gifts? *(Allow for guesses.)* Yes, some of you may have a stepdad, but today I'm remembering that each of us has an earthly dad and a heavenly Father. When Jesus talked about his Father in Heaven, he reminded us that his Father is our Father too. The Bible tells us that we have a Father in Heaven who loves us and takes care of us. He will always be with us—even when our other dad is not around.

I tried very hard to find a gift that both my fathers would want. What do you think would be the best gift for our Father in Heaven? *(Love.)* I think that is exactly what our dads on earth want too. Our love is the perfect gift, and it can be given with any other gift you might have.

On this Father's Day, remember to tell both your fathers how much you love them.

PRAYER:

Thank you, God, for our dads and for being our Father in Heaven. Help us to show our love for you and for the dads you have given us. Amen.

FOURTH OF JULY
CELEBRATE FREEDOM

THEME: Freedom in Christ

OBJECTS: Sparkler, matches

TEXT: I will obey your teachings forever and ever. So I will live in freedom because I want to follow your orders.   *Psalm 119:44, 45*

APPLICATION:

The Fourth of July is a time of celebration. What do we celebrate? *(Freedom for our country.)* In what ways do we celebrate the Fourth? *(Discuss.)* I love to watch fireworks, but I especially like to celebrate with sparklers. The darker it is, the brighter they shine. *(Demonstrate.)* It's fun to wave them around and then carefully light another before the first one goes out.

As Christians, we have a special reason to celebrate. Not only is our country free, but we are also free in Christ. You might think being a Christian gives you some pretty hard rules about things you should and should not do. But we need to remember that loving Jesus gives us great freedom. Can you think of any ways you have freedom because you belong to Jesus? *(Responses.)* For one thing, we can be set free from guilt because if we are truly sorry when we do something wrong, and ask God to forgive us, he does! We are also free to say no to temptation. With Jesus in our hearts, we don't have to sin. You and I are free to choose whether we will do good or bad things. We can also be free from worrying about the future because we belong to Jesus and know that he will always take care of us. Even when bad things happen to us, we don't have to worry, because Jesus will always be with us to help us.

When we see a sparkler, we are reminded of the freedom of our country—but Christians should also be reminders of the freedom we have in Christ. The darker things may be, the more you and I should shine with the light of Jesus that can be passed on to others.

Let's celebrate that our country has freedom, and that we belong to Jesus, the one who gives us the greatest freedom of all.

PRAYER:

Lord, we give thanks for a free country, and praise you for the freedom we have in you. Amen.

BLOWING BUBBLES

THEME: God's power within us

OBJECT: Bubble gum

TEXT: This is my work, and I can do it only because Christ's mighty energy is at work within me.
Colossians 1:29, TLB

APPLICATION:

I love bubble gum and I love to blow bubbles! Who knows how to blow bubbles? Let me show you how I do it. *(Demonstrate.)* First, I chew the bubble gum until it is soft; then I make a dent in it with my tongue. It's not easy, but if there are no holes, I can blow into it and make a big, beautiful bubble.

(Hold up a new piece of fresh gum.) Could you make a bubble out of this without chewing it to make it soft and then blowing air into it? *(No.)* Blowing a bubble can seem like hard work, but I like this kind of work, don't you? After all our efforts and practice, we can become really good at blowing bubbles!

This weekend we celebrate Labor Day. The holiday reminds us how good it is to be able to work. Even if we are too young to go away to a job, we all have work to do at school, and chores to do at home. How does it feel when we work really hard at something and know we've done our best? *(Good.)* We feel especially good when we get a good grade or a compliment for a job well done. What if we weren't able to work and accomplish these things? What if we didn't have the ability in our minds to remember information or the physical strength to walk or lift things with our arms?

Today, we need to remember that just as it takes our breath to make a big, beautiful bubble, we couldn't do anything without the energy God puts inside us, or the ability he gives us. And if we give God control and let his power work through us, we can do even more than we ever dreamed possible! He never gets tired, and he always gives us the right amount of energy to do what we need to do. So make your heart soft for God and let him fill you with his energy.

PRAYER:

Dear God, our work is a blessing from you. Take control, and give us your energy to do a good job in everything we do. Amen.

"PURR-FECT" PRAISE

THEME: Giving thanks

OBJECT: Kitten (can be a toy)

TEXT: You changed my sorrow into dancing. You took away my rough cloth, which shows sadness, and clothed me in happiness.

Psalm 30:11

APPLICATION:

What does a kitten do when it is given food, love, or warmth—when it's happy? *(It purrs.)* Some say that the only time a cat purrs is when someone is around. I'm not sure if that's true or not—I just know that it makes me feel good when I make a cat happy enough to purr. You might say that purring is a cat's special way of saying thanks.

Just as a kitten is happy and content when we care for it, we also are happy and content when God gives us food, love, and everything we need. How do we let him know we are thankful? *(Responses.)* Sometimes we forget and don't let him know. But we should say thanks at least as loudly and naturally as a kitten. We may not purr, but there are many other ways we can give thanks. Can you think of some ways we can thank God out loud? *(Singing, whistling, praying aloud, etc.)*

God is always there to hear our thanks, and he is always happy when we give it!

PRAYER:

Dear Heavenly Father, how thankful we are for all you do for us. Help us to remember to give you thanks every day! Amen.

COME IN

THEME: Come with thanksgiving.

OBJECT: "No Trespassing" sign—(On the reverse side print, "Come In")

TEXT: Come into his city with songs of thanksgiving. Come into his courtyards with songs of praise. Thank him, and praise his name.

Psalm 100:4

APPLICATION:

I like to go for walks in the woods. It's fun to explore. Yet, just as I get ready to climb a fence, I may see a sign that says: "No Trespassing." *(Show sign.)* What does that mean? *(Responses.)* If you see a "No Trespassing" sign, you must keep out. Even though I may want to go in and walk through woods, or smell the flowers, the area belongs to someone who wants me to stay out, so that's what I have to do.

But you know what? There isn't a "No Trespassing" sign on the place where God lives. He asks that we come into *(flip to reverse side of sign)* his home often, with thanksgiving for all he gives. Our church building is one of the places we can go to meet with God. In fact, we sometimes call it "God's house." He wants to be with us there, and he never puts up a "No Trespassing" sign. He doesn't want to keep us out; he wants us to come in and be with him. No one ever has to stay on the outside looking in. Everyone is welcome. We can enjoy spending time with God and thank him for everything he does for us!

PRAYER:

God, we want to say thanks for always inviting us to come into your house. Amen.

GET REALLY READY

THEME: Prepare for Jesus.

OBJECT: A computer disc

TEXT: "John said, Change your hearts and lives because the kingdom of heaven is coming soon.' John the Baptist is the one Isaiah the prophet was talking about. Isaiah said: 'This is a voice of a man who calls out in the desert: "Prepare the way for the Lord. Make the road straight for him."'"
Matthew 3:2, 3

APPLICATION:

Do any of you play games or do homework on the computer? *(Yes.)* A computer can be lots of fun when it works. Mine often freezes up. I move my mouse to the left or slide it to the right but nothing happens on the monitor. Other times the computer sends my work to such a safe place I can't find it again. When I tried to save some good stuff on this disc *(show)*, the screen told me it was full. I just wanted to have fun. Now, to make things right, I have to empty this disc so I can save better stuff. I get really frustrated. It's a good thing I have friends who can help me solve computer problems.

Just like playing on the computer, Christmas can also be lots of fun. What kinds of things are you doing as you get ready to celebrate the birth of Jesus? *(Discuss.)* Are you busy wrapping presents? Did your tree get decorated? Christmastime can be full and frustrating. When I plug in the bottom string of lights on the tree, the top one goes out. I once bought my aunt a blouse in a large size before I noticed that she had stopped eating candy and had lost a lot of weight! That was embarrassing! And did you know that Poinsettia flowers are poisonous to your cat? Yep, Christmas can be pretty hectic.

Fortunately, there is help. The Bible tells us what is really necessary to make room for Jesus. Like cleaning computer discs, we need to remove what does not belong in our lives. We may want to concentrate on having fun, but before celebrating Jesus' birth we need to say we are sorry for the bad things we have done and get rid of everything that keeps us from serving Jesus. The Bible calls that repenting. If we repent, Jesus will forgive our sins and we will be really ready for Christmas.

PRAYER:

Lord, help us prepare for celebrating the birth of Jesus by being sorry for what we have done wrong, and deciding to serve you better. Amen.

A GiFT FoR GoD

THEME: Salvation; giving ourselves to God

OBJECT: A gift-wrapped mirror

TEXT: Since God has shown us great mercy, I beg you to offer your lives as a living sacrifice to him. Your offering must be only for God and pleasing to him.
Romans 12:1

APPLiCATioN:

I love to give gifts at Christmastime! Have you ever given a gift to some-one that made him or her *very* happy? *(Give examples.)*

Today I tried to find a gift that I could give to God. We sometimes forget that although God made everything and doesn't need any gifts from us, there is a gift we can give him that makes him very happy. In fact, I think I found just the *gift (hold up present)* that would make God most happy. What do you think it might be? *(Responses.)* Let's open the box, and see what is. *(Open box and let someone see inside.)* What do you see when you look inside? *(Answer: mirror—"who's in the mirror?" Me, I am.)*

The best gift we can give to God is ourselves. Jesus gave his life for us to free us from sin and give us eternal life. There was no greater gift he could have given us! And when we give ourselves to him, we join his family and it makes him so glad!

So make yourself God's Christmas present. You don't have to wrap your-self up; just ask him to live in your heart. It's the best gift you can ever give to him.

PRAYER:

Dear God, we give ourselves as gifts to you. Thank you for letting us be part of your family. Amen.

OPEN THE GiFT

THEME: Accept God's gift.

OBJECTS: Wrapped box containing double candy canes—enough for each child to have one. (To make double candy canes, using either mini or regular-size candy canes, tape two together to make a heart shape: ♡).

TEXT: Thanks be to God for his gift that is too wonderful to explain.

2 Corinthians 9:15

APPLiCATiON:

Christmas is a wonderful time of the year for a lot of reasons. What do you like best about Christmas? *(List a number of things until the giving of gifts is mentioned.)* No doubt about it, one of the things that makes Christmas so special is the giving of gifts. I brought along a beautiful gift for us to look at. Don't you love the pretty paper and big bow? It's for all of us, so let's set it right in the middle of our group so we can watch it. *(Spend a little time watching it.)*

Well, that's about it, I guess. Thank you for sitting so quietly. Is there anything else we should do? *(Kids will want to open it.)* You want to open it? We all want to open the present. I can hardly wait!

Even though we are usually anxious to open gifts given to us, we are all given a very special gift that some people never open. God loved us so much, he gave us the gift of Jesus. We have to believe in him and accept him into our hearts. Yet, some never take that step and they miss out on the greatest gift anyone ever gave us.

(Speak as opening gift.) God's gift of love to each of us is salvation. Jesus died on a cross so each of us can have that salvation—the gift of eternal life. *(Hand out heart-shaped candy canes.)*

Christmas is a time to remember the most incredible gift of all. Jesus came to earth as a baby, but also as our Savior. If you have not opened his gift of love and accepted Jesus into your heart, it's not too late—you can do so today.

PRAYER:

God, I want to open the gift you have given me. I want Jesus to be my Savior and my Lord. Amen.

THE STRAIGHT MESSAGE

THEME: Christmas is about Jesus' birth.

OBJECT: Curling ribbon

TEXT: Today your Savior was born in David's town. He is Christ, the Lord.
Luke 2:11

APPLICATION:

Christmas is special because we celebrate a very special birthday. Whose birthday do we celebrate? *(Jesus'.)* That's right! In fact, without Jesus, there would be no Christmas. But sometimes people forget about that.

I've brought along some ribbon today that reminds me of what has happened to the celebration of Christmas. The Christmas message, just like this ribbon, is very straight and simple: Jesus our Savior was born. Now when we scrape the ribbon like this *(demonstrate)*, something happens to it. See how it is possible to change the ribbon into something very different? Instead of being straight, it curls up and winds all over the place.

Christmas has seemed to change too. It is no longer simply a celebration of the birth of Jesus. People have added all kinds of other things. Santa Claus, elves, Christmas trees, reindeer, and presents are all now a part of the celebration. When we focus on these things, it's easy to forget about the greatest gift of all—Jesus.

But you know what? You can help straighten out the message of Christmas. *(Run your scissors over the reverse side of the ribbon until it is straight again.)* Remember that Christmas honors the day that Jesus our Savior was born. Make sure your friends understand that too. And when you open your gifts, remember that Jesus is the greatest gift we've ever received!

PRAYER:

God, help us to remember the straight message of Christmas—that Jesus our Savior was born. Amen.

POWER PACKED

THEME: Being filled with God's power

OBJECTS: Two balloons: one that has to be blown up, and one that has been blown up, tied, and has become old, limp, deflated

TEXT: Our physical body is becoming older and weaker, but our spirit inside us is made new every day.   *2 Corinthians 4:16*

APPLICATION:

I love balloons, don't you? A lot of people celebrate the end of a year with balloons. What is the best way to see a balloon—when it's empty and flat like this *(hold up first balloon)* or when it's big and full of air? *(Responses.)* When blown up, balloons are light and bright. *(Blow up first balloon.)* Tell me, what happens when the balloon sits around for several days? *(Responses.)* Right! It slowly loses air until it looks like this *(show limp and deflated balloon).* What happens when you blow up a balloon and then let go of it? *(Responses.)* You don't want to see me do that now, do you? Well, OK. *(Let the inflated balloon go.)* All the air inside is gone, just like that! *(Snap fingers.)*

You know, just as our lungs fill the balloon up with air, when we have Jesus inside us, we are filled up with his power! His power changes us, helping us to be more like him. And just as we need to keep adding air to fill a balloon, we need to keep adding Jesus to our lives. What are some ways we can do this? *(Discuss.)* Going to church and Sunday school, reading his Word, and talking to him are all ways to keep ourselves filled with God's power. If we don't stay filled, we will begin to look like this old, deflated balloon that has laid around too long.

What happens when we do something mean and wicked on purpose? God's power leaves us quickly just like the balloon that we let go of earlier. Why? Because God is good and his power will not stay within a person who chooses to sin. That is why we must ask for God's forgiveness when we sin, so that his power will come back into our lives. This is important to remember at this time of the year. It's not just the end of an old year, but the beginning of a new year. Don't be caught without your power. Continue doing those things that keep you filled up with Jesus and ask him to be the power source in your life every day.

PRAYER:

Lord, keep filling us with you so we will always have your power in our lives. Amen.

SEALED AND DELIVERED

THEME: Belonging to God

OBJECTS: Wax, a seal, a self-sealing envelope

TEXT: "He put his mark on us to show that we are his. And he put his Spirit in our hearts to be a guarantee for all he has promised."

2 Corinthians 1:22

APPLICATION:

Do you like to get mail? It's fun to open the envelopes and see what is inside, isn't it? But it's not as much fun to get a letter ready to mail—especially when it's time to lick the envelope. That glue usually tastes horrible. That's the bad news. The good news is that licking the shiny stuff on the flap makes it sticky enough to keep the envelope closed *(demonstrate)*. That's a good deal. It keeps the pictures we send grandmas and grandpas from falling out, and it keeps others from reading what we wrote.

Did you know that before envelopes were made with glue on the flap, people figured out a way to seal the envelopes? I've brought along some wax to show you how envelopes were once sealed. After the wax was melted, it was pressed with a seal *(demonstrate)*. By looking carefully at the seal you could tell who sent the letter. Ownership was shown with a design or initials.

Just as a seal shows who wrote a letter, baptism is also a sign that shows ownership. When you are baptized, you receive the Holy Spirit, God's seal on you (Acts 2:38). God's seal reminds us of the special bond we have with our Lord Jesus Christ. Just as the wax seal protects what is inside of the envelope, the Holy Spirit protects us and marks us a members of God's family.

PRAYER:

Lord God, we celebrate the love you have for us. Thank you for setting your seal of ownership on us when we are baptized. Amen.

COLOR iT NEW

THEME: In Christ we are a new creation.

OBJECTS: White cardboard, yellow and blue markers

TEXT: "If anyone belongs to Christ, then he is made new. The old things have gone; everything is made new!"   *2 Corinthians 5:17*

APPLICATION:

I love to put colors on paper. See how pretty blue looks when I put it on this white paper? *(Color a wide swath of blue marker on one side of the white cardboard.)* Another great color is yellow. See how bright it looks next to the blue? *(Color some yellow next to the blue.)* And that is not all! Something awesome happens when I mix these two colors. *(Color yellow over some of the blue to make green.)* Look at the green we get when the blue is mixed with the yellow. Green is my favorite color. It reminds me of beautiful grass and the leaves on flowers growing in my garden.

The Bible tells us that something awesome happens when we accept Jesus as our Savior. We have new life. Just like the blue and yellow combined to make a brand new color *(point)*, when Jesus touches our lives we become totally new. He changes how we act. Remember the pretty green color that came when we blended blue and yellow? The result of blending our lives with Jesus is even more beautiful. What things might change when Jesus comes into your heart? *(Discuss examples such as wanting to obey God, telling others about Jesus, not using bad words, etc.)*

The green on our paper *(point)* is so pretty it is the first thing I see when I look at the paper. Others should know right away—you have new life because of Jesus Christ. Everyone should be able to see that Jesus is in your heart.

PRAYER:

Jesus, when we love you we become totally new. Thank you for that wonderful change. Amen.

BIBLE STUDY
LIVING BY THE BOOK

THEME: God's Word keeps us pure.

OBJECTS: A thermos, a glass of milk, and a Bible

TEXT: "How can a young person live a pure life? He can do it by obeying your word." *Psalm 119:9*

APPLICATION:

I thought I might get thirsty this morning, so I brought along an ice cold glass of milk. Nothing beats cold milk for quenching your thirst. *(Take a sip.)* Humm . . . *(frown).* Yuck! This milk is warm and a little sour. What a disappointment! Of course, I couldn't very well bring a whole refrigerator with me. How else could I have kept it cold? *(Discuss.)* Some of you already noticed this thermos. If I had put my milk inside, it would have stayed fresh and cold. Have you ever used a thermos? *(Yes.)* How does it work? If I take it apart *(demonstrate)* I can see that it has a liner inside that keeps my milk cold or my soup hot. Without a thermos, it is impossible to keep my food fresh and tasting good.

There are many times when—like my sour milk—we are not the best we could be. Maybe we pick fights with others, or talk back to parents and teachers. We may be tempted to take something that does not belong to us. A whole church full of Christians could help us behave, but just as we can't carry around a whole refrigerator, we can't have an entire church with us all the time either. Even dragging only the pastor along would not be easy.

The Bible is our answer. *(Hold up Bible.)* Being close to a thermos didn't help my milk stay cold. You can't just put a Bible on the chair next to you—you have to do what it says. That's why Sunday school and Bible studies are so important. When we learn what the Bible teaches we can follow its directions. Without knowing the Bible it is impossible to keep our lives pure and honoring to God.

PRAYER:

Dear Lord, we want to be good boys and girls. Help us follow the directions you give us the Bible. Amen.

COMMISSION
Go To iT!

THEME: Equipping for service

OBJECTS: Bricks, helium balloons, and the participation of a person who is going into some kind of Christian service.

TEXT: "I pray that the God of peace will give you every good thing you need so that you can do what he wants."   *Hebrews 13:20*

APPLicATioN:

What an exciting day! Today I get to introduce Pastor Smith who is coming to work at our church. *(You might introduce someone who is going to a mission field or a short term Christian endeavor.)* Let's talk about our part in getting him started in this new job.

I brought him a welcome gift *(or something to take with him)*. These bricks will be nice for him to have don't you think? *(As bricks are being passed to the pastor he may exaggerate the weight by slumping beneath the load.)* Won't these heavy bricks be a big help to him? *(No.)* No? Why not? *(While you take back the bricks, discuss.)* I guess you're right. It would be hard to carry around these bricks, and the weight might even hurt him.

I also brought along some balloons. They are filled with helium. I have to hang on tight, because they want lift right up toward the ceiling. *(Tuck them under the pastor's arms as you talk.)* Is this better to give than the bricks? Why? *(Discuss/lighten his load.)* The balloons could cheer him up and make his days easier. We might have to be careful not to overdue it. *(Pause and look up.)*

The point is that we can make Pastor Smith's life hard—just as if we were adding bricks to his load. We could be unfriendly, or give him all the work we should be doing ourselves. We could refuse to support any of his new ideas.

It would be much better to make his job easier. How can we do that? *(Share ideas.)* We might send him a note or draw him a picture. Let him know your name so you can be friends. You could share a candy bar. Most of all, pray that God will bless his work. You can make Pastor Smith's load lighter—like giving him balloons instead of bricks.

PRAYER:

Lord, bless Pastor Smith and be with him and with us as we serve you together. Amen.

EVANGELISM
BENDABLE HELPERS

THEME: Putting others first

OBJECTS: A regular straw and a flexible straw

TEXT: Love each other like brothers and sisters. Give your brothers and sisters more honor than you want for yourselves. . . . Share with God's people who need help. Bring strangers in need into your homes.

Romans 12:10, 13

APPLICATION:

I really enjoy drinking beverages through a straw. In fact, I use one every time I get a chance. Sometimes it's not easy to drink from a regular straw. If I am lying down, it's nearly impossible to drink from a regular straw without spilling everything. *(Show how hard it is to reach.)* But there is a different kind of straw that can bend *(demonstrate)*. This is a flexible straw. With this kind of straw, I can easily get a drink, even if I'm lying down.

Today I want to talk about bending. To help us get a drink, the straw has to bend. And sometimes, to help others get what they need, we have to bend too. How can we do this? *(Responses.)* God tells us to share with others. Sometimes that means we must put their needs ahead of our own. You may need to give part of your lunch to someone who doesn't have any lunch. You may need to talk to that kid at school who no one else will talk to. You may need to give up your seat on the bus to someone who needs to sit down more than you do. We need to be willing to tell others about Jesus Christ. We may feel a little embarrassed to talk about Jesus to someone who does not know about God. It may seem easier for us to just not say anything. You may not feel like doing any of these things. Do you think the Bible means that we must share with everyone, or just the people we really like? *(Discuss.)*

Not only does God want us to share, but he wants us to do it lovingly. That's not always easy. Loving means bending—being willing to bend like this flexible straw. Let's try to remember to be giving and helpful to others, even when it's uncomfortable or inconvenient—even when we have to bend a bit.

PRAYER:

God, help us to be willing to bend—even if it means going out of our way to share with others. Amen.

ARMED TO SERVE

> **THEME:** Serving others
>
> **OBJECTS:** Crackers
>
> **TEXT:** Serve each other with love. The whole law is made complete in this one command: "Love your neighbor as you love yourself."
>
> *Galatians 5:13, 14*

APPLICATION:

Once upon a time, there was a land called No-Elbows. You know about *(your state)* and you've heard of *(a state near yours)*. But have you heard of the state of No-Elbows? Probably not. What do you suppose the people of No-Elbows are like? *(Allow discussion leading to the fact that they have no elbows. Show what your arm would be like without an elbow.)*

The people in No-Elbows were divided into two groups. The No-Elbow-Lights were thin, weak, and sickly. They had a lot of trouble eating. How would you eat if you had no elbows? I'm going to give each of you a cracker and let's see how you do in feeding yourselves. Now, don't bend your elbows! *(Give out crackers and let the children discover the difficulty getting things in their mouths without bending their elbows.)*

The other group, the No-Elbows-Kin, were strong and healthy. How do you suppose they ate? *(Allow for guessing, demonstrating a few possibilities— tossing the crackers up, and trying to catch them in your mouth. Lead to the fact that they fed each other.)* When the No-Elbows-Kin fed each other, they were giving to someone else—and thinking about the needs of others over their own. That's what the Bible means when it says, "Love your neighbor as you love yourself."

God tells us in his Word that he wants us to love each other, and show that love by helping each other. We can share with those who live close to us, as well as with those who live far away. When we think about the needs of others, and give of ourselves to them, we are loving them the way God has taught us to in his Word.

PRAYER:

God, may our love for others be shown in our helping each other. Amen.

VISITORS

WARMLY WELCOME

THEME: Warm welcome

OBJECTS: Scarves, coats, mittens, gloves

TEXT: Warmly welcome each other into the church, just as Christ has warmly welcomed you; then God will be glorified.

Romans 15:7, TLB

APPLICATION:

Today I picked a special Bible verse to share with you. Romans 15:7 tells us to "warmly welcome each other into the church." *(Repeat the verse aloud together.)*

I want to do everything right, so I've brought extra coats and hats for all of you. *(Hand out warm clothes.)* Let's see. Will these mittens fit you? Yes, that looks good. Here, this scarf matches your dress. This pair of gloves will fit you. *(Continue until all articles are passed out.)*

Well, what do you think? The Bible tells me to warmly welcome each of you. Did I do well? *(Pause.)* What? You don't think this is what is meant by warmly welcoming each other? You're right. What must we do to warmly welcome each other?

To "warmly welcome" is to be friendly and helpful, to make others feel comfortable. How can we do that? *(Discuss ways.)* Yes, you can introduce yourself to people you don't know. Talk to new people, and have them meet your friends. Help visitors find Sunday school classes, and share your Bible or your songbook. It's not easy to go by yourself to a new place, and it helps if others are kind to you and help you find your way around.

The Bible says when we warmly welcome others into our church, God is glorified. What does that mean? *(We bring honor to him, praise him, show others a little bit of what God is like.)* God has warmly welcomed us into his church. We should just as warmly welcome others.

I'll take back all of the warm clothes now, but I hope you will all remember to give God's kind of warm welcome to others who come to worship with us.

PRAYER:

Lord, you have welcomed us to worship you. Help us to welcome others into your church. Amen.

HE LOVES ME

THEME: God's love

OBJECTS: Two daisies

TEXT: Give thanks to the Lord because he is good. His love continues forever. *Psalm 136:1*

APPLICATION:

When I was young, I had a little game I played to find out if someone loved me. Maybe you've tried this too. Just find a flower, and begin to pull out the petals one by one. *(Demonstrate pulling out a petal with each phrase.)* He loves me . . . he loves me not . . . he loves me . . . he loves me not. The last petal gives me the answer I'm stuck with. If I don't want that answer, I need to pick another flower. The only problem with this is that it's only a game—it doesn't really let me know if that person loves me. It is only a guess.

But when it comes to the question of God's love for us, there's no guessing. God's love for us is so certain that there is no need to pull out any petals. His love is shown in the wonderful world he created for us, in the food that he has given us, in the abilities that he has blessed us with, in the help that he gives us every day. Most of all, his love is shown in sending Jesus to be our Savior. When it comes to God's love, we can say with every petal *(demonstrate with the second daisy),* he loves us . . . he loves us . . . he loves us. How wonderful it is to know that God always loves us!

PRAYER:

Thank you, God, for your love that never changes and never ends. Amen.

THE SMiLiNG TURTLE

THEME: God's protection

OBJECTS: A turtle

TEXT: Protect me, God, because I trust in you. . . . The Lord is all I need. He takes care of me.
Psalm 16:1, 5

APPLiCATiON:

If you wander around a lake or a creek, you may see a turtle. If he is not in the water, you can easily catch him because turtles can't run fast. Do you know what the turtle does when he is scared? *(Discuss his protective shell.)* Have you noticed that even though he can't move fast on the ground, the turtle can get inside his shell in a flash? With his feet, head, and tail out of reach, he feels safe. Pick the turtle up and look at his face. His little mouth curls just a bit on each side. You may think it is my imagination, but inside his shell, the turtle seems to be smiling.

We don't have a shell to pull into like this turtle, but we can be thankful that we still have protection. If we belong to Jesus, he is there to help us when we are afraid. Just as the turtle can pull quickly into his shell, we can ask Jesus to give us the safety and protection we need. Are you ever scared? *(Discuss.)* I think we all are scared sometimes. But God gives us people we can go to when we're frightened—a parent, a teacher, or another adult you can trust. And we can always ask God for his help when we feel we are in danger. Let's take another look at the turtle. Remember how we can see him smile when he is safe? We can be just as happy and secure when we put our trust in Jesus.

PRAYER:

Dear God, thank you for always being there when we call. Keep us safe and help us to trust in your protection. Amen.

SPRING

GOD IS EVERYWHERE

THEME: God is always with us.

OBJECT: Pussy willow branch (may be artificial)

TEXT: I can *never* get away from my God! . . . If I ride the morning winds to the farthest oceans, even there your hand will guide me, your strength will support me. If I try to hide in the darkness, the night becomes light around me. For even darkness cannot hide from God.
Psalm 139: 7, 9-12, TLB

APPLICATION:

I brought a special kind of branch with me today—does anyone know what this is? *(Responses.)* That's right—it's a pussy willow branch. If you walk in certain areas of the woods, you might see pussy willow bushes. It's not unusual to see a bush in the woods, but this kind of bush is different. Spaced on the branches are little furry balls, as soft as a kitten. See? *(Allow children to feel the softness of the buds.)* Who would believe it? Fur on a bush! What an unlikely place to find little bunches of fur!

Just as we might not expect to find fur on a bush, there are some places we might not expect to find God. Would we find God in the woods? *(Allow children to respond to each question.)* How about at your school? Is he at your house? Is he here? Suppose I wanted to hide from God. If I turned off all the lights on a very dark night, do you think he could still see me, or find me? *(Discuss.)* Where can you go that God wouldn't be? *(Discuss—nowhere.)*

The Bible tells us that God will always be near to guide us and help us. There is no place that we would ever be that God would not be there with us. We might be surprised to find fur on a pussy willow bush, but knowing God is with us everywhere is no surprise. He promises to always guide us and give us his strength wherever we may go.

PRAYER:

We thank you, Lord, for always being with us no matter where we are. Amen.

DON'T GET BURNED

THEME: Pride

OBJECTS: Marshmallows: white, toasted, and burned, or marshmallows with a candle or a campfire

TEXT: Pride will destroy a person. A proud attitude leads to ruin.
Proverbs 16:18

APPLICATION:

Marshmallows *(show)* are so-o-o good to eat, especially if roasted over a fire. As they heat, they start to slowly puff up. If you're very careful, you can roast them to a beautiful golden brown *(show)*—and they taste delicious! But be careful—if you hold them too close to the fire, or keep them over the fire too long, they can burn, and then they taste terrible!

You know, people are kind of like marshmallows too. When something good happens to us, or we do something very well, we feel warm and good, like the marshmallow roasted to a golden brown. If we remember that everything we have or are able to do is a gift from God, this is a good feeling. But we can also become too proud, and once we get warmed up, we just keep on bragging. If we act like we're better than everyone else, people don't like to be around us. Like the marshmallow left over the fire too long, when we become too puffed up, the results are pretty bad *(show burned marshmallow)*.

The Bible warns us about pride. It can lead to our getting hurt, or our hurting others. Worst of all, it causes us to act just the opposite of how Jesus wants us to be—kind and humble. We should focus on him more than we focus on ourselves.

Be careful not to let good feelings turn into a pride that leads to losing friends, and not giving God the credit for what he has done in our lives. God gives us the ability to do everything we accomplish. Let's always try to remember that and not get burned by our own pride.

PRAYER:

Lord, keep us humble, knowing everything we have is a wonderful gift from you. Amen.

FiRED UP

THEME: Salvation is a gift.

OBJECTS: Two sticks

TEXT: Salvation is not a reward for the good we have done, so none of us can take any credit for it. It is God himself who has made us what we are and given us new lives from Christ Jesus.

Ephesians 2:9, 10, TLB

APPLiCATiON:

Have you ever gone camping? What are some of the things you might do if you go camping? *(Responses.)* When I go camping, after putting up my tent and setting up all my gear, I usually make a campfire. I always use matches, but I've heard that a fire can also be started by rubbing two sticks together. Did you know that? Imagine being able to start a fire with just two sticks. Do you think I could do it? *(Responses.)*

(Hold up the two sticks.) All I have to do is rub these together. You watch for signs of smoke and sparks, OK? *(Begin rubbing.)* Does anyone see a fire? *(Rub some more.)* I think it is warmer here. Do you feel it? No? *(Rub faster.)* Does anyone smell smoke? *(Sniff.)*

This doesn't seem to be working. I've never actually started a fire this way. In fact, very few people can. Do you know anyone who can start a fire by rubbing sticks together? You really have to know what you're doing. You have to be a master at outdoor camping skills. I can keep on working at it, and trying to do everything just right, but I won't be able to get this fire started with these sticks—no matter how hard I try.

You know, being a Christian can be like that. Just as I tried to be a great fire-maker, I can try hard to do everything right in my life, and be very good all the time, so I will get into Heaven someday. But nothing I do will ever be good enough. Accepting Jesus into our hearts is the only true way into Heaven. Let's thank him for dying on the cross to save us and make it possible for us to have eternal life.

PRAYER:

Jesus, thank you for giving your life so that we can have salvation. Amen.

LET'S STICK TOGETHER

THEME: Unity; working together

OBJECTS: S'more ingredients: graham crackers, marshmallows, flat chocolate candy bars; campfire, grill, or candle flame

TEXT: Patience and encouragement come from God. And I pray that God will help you all agree with each other the way Christ Jesus wants.
Romans 15:5

APPLICATION:

I know why my favorite campfire treat is called a "s'more." When you eat one, you must have some more! What could be better? Crunchy graham crackers, chocolate, and marshmallows are all treats in themselves. The taste of all three melted together is scrumptious!

Let's make one! *(Lead children in making s'mores.)* First, we need one of these graham cracker squares. Then we'll take half of this chocolate bar and set it on top. Then we add the warm, toasted marshmallow and another layer of graham cracker, and smush the whole snack together! Delicious! Let's take a bite!

This sounds simple, but it's hard to make a perfect s'more. If you leave the marshmallow over the fire too long, it becomes a torch that you have to blow out. *(May demonstrate.)* If you don't get the marshmallow close enough to the fire, it won't get warm and melt, and you won't be able to squeeze the s'more enough to get your mouth around it.

But when you get it just right, it is a very tasty experience! The golden brown, warm marshmallow melts the chocolate, and they become one yummy layer between the crispy cracker! The flavor is much better than a graham cracker, or a marshmallow, or chocolate by itself, isn't it?

You know, just like all the different parts of a s'more have to blend together to make this yummy treat, so do we, as Christians, need to come together and agree to live as Jesus wants us to live. He wants us to be patient with each other and encourage one another too. What are some ways we can do this? *(Responses.)*

When we work together and get along with each other, we have a spirit of unity. Sometimes things happen to hurt us and we build hard shells around ourselves. When we do that, our shell may keep us from getting close to others. Sometimes, like the cold marshmallow, we stay away from others who are different than we are—or others who we just don't like. *(Demonstrate how the hard marshmallow keeps the two graham crackers apart.)* But God wants us to fit together with others and be helpful to them. Just as the warm marshmallow melts the chocolate, the warm love of Jesus inside us can help us get along with others in our church and family. It isn't always easy, but together we can do it—and our unity will draw us closer to each other, and closer to Jesus.

PRAYER:

Lord, give us a spirit of unity. May we grow close to each other, so that together we can serve you better. Amen.

SUMMER

A PERFECT FiT

THEME: Praise

OBJECTS: A hot dog and hot dog bun, a hamburger and hamburger bun.

TEXT: Praise the Lord. How good it is to sing praises to our God, how pleasant and fitting to praise him!

Psalm 147:1

APPLICATION:

The best part of having a cookout is the smell of the hot dogs and hamburgers on the grill. The smell makes your mouth water and your stomach growl. I can hardly wait for the meat to be put on the buns, so I can pour on ketchup, mustard, and all the other goopy stuff. Tell me, do the hamburgers go on this long bun, or do they go on the round one? Can't the hamburgers go on the hot dog bun? Why not? Let's try it. *(Put it on the wrong bun.)* Hmm. This doesn't really work. Let's try the hot dog on the hamburger bun. *(Put hot dog on hamburger bun.)* This is even worse. Suppose I made a hamburger in the shape of a hot dog bun, or cut up a hot dog to fit a round bun. Would that seem strange? *(Yes.)* So what you're saying is that hot dog buns are made to fit hot dogs, and hamburger buns are the perfect match for hamburgers. The buns are made for that purpose.

Did you ever stop to think that just like buns, we are made for a certain purpose? The Bible talks about what we are made to do. We are made to praise God. In fact, not praising him is just as strange as putting a hot dog on a hamburger bun. We may try to reshape ourselves, and forget about praising Jesus for who he is and all he's done, but something will be missing in our lives—something will feel like a bad fit. As Christians, praising God should be as natural as breathing—as normal as a hamburger or hot dog fitting into the right bun—because that's what we are made to do!

PRAYER:

Lord, may we always remember why we were made, and gratefully praise you. Amen.

SUMMER
SURROUNDED

THEME: God's surrounding love

OBJECT: Life jacket

TEXT: Wicked people have many troubles. But the Lord's love surrounds those who trust him.
Psalm 32:10

APPLICATION:

On a hot summer day it's great to go swimming! What are some places where people go swimming? *(Ocean, lake, pond, swimming pool, etc.)* No matter how good a swimmer I am, when I go out into deep water, I wear a life jacket. I put it around me like this *(demonstrate),* and no matter what rough waves come my way, I always feel safe. That doesn't mean I'm always comfortable. Sometimes the jacket feels tight or it floats up under my chin—and I can't move as freely as I might without it, but these are small things to put up with, considering the wonderful ride I enjoy bouncing along on each swell of a wave.

Just as we are wrapped in safety when we wear life jackets, the Lord's love surrounds and protects each of us when we belong to him. Oh, we may still have some rough times in life, but we know we won't drown when we have Jesus to surround us with his love and care. His love will protect and keep us safe in those rough times.

Sometimes we feel that love when friends he has given to love us put their arms around us in comforting hugs. We can just relax, and let Jesus take care of us, because we know he has everything under control.

PRAYER:

Lord, what a joy it is to rest in you, surrounded by your love. Amen.

TAKE ACTION

THEME: Faith without works

OBJECT: Water toboggan or tube

TEXT: So you see that a person is made right with God by the things he does. He cannot be made right by faith only. . . . Faith that does nothing is dead!   *James 2:24, 26*

APPLICATION:

I can't wait to try out my new water toboggan (or inner tube)! Let's put it down here in the middle of us. I think it will hold me without a problem, so I'll just take this towrope, and drape it over the side, like this. *(Put it over the side of the tube.)* Then I'll just relax in the tube (on the toboggan) and grab the towrope. I've been told to hold on very tight.

(Sit a few seconds. Move around a little, and sit a few seconds more.) Hmm. This experience is certainly not all it's cracked up to be. What am I doing wrong? Yes, I'm teasing you. I could sit here all day just resting in the comfort of this tube, and nothing will ever happen. I need to do some things. What do I need to do? *(Discuss.)*

First, I must go to the right place—such as a lake—to use my toboggan. But even then nothing will happen unless I hook the toboggan up to a powerboat. Once it is hooked up, all I have to do is tell the driver to "hit it," and he'll take off—then I'll have the fun, exciting ride I want to have! If I don't take action to do these important things first, I can forget about enjoying my water toboggan!

This reminds me of how we sometimes live our lives. Just as I just sat in the tube waiting for things to happen, too often, because I belong to Jesus, I just sit back and do nothing—waiting for others to do things for God.

The Bible says that when our faith is alive we show it by our actions. Just as we take our water toboggan to the lake where it can be used, we must also go where God can put us to work. Just as my toboggan must be hooked up to the boat, we have to get hooked up to God's power. Without that power we can never do what God wants us to do. We also need to let him know that we are ready and willing to do what pleases him. Then we must live our lives serving him.

What kinds of things can we do to show that we love God? *(Discuss ways: helping others, telling others about Jesus, being kind, etc.)*

After we have hooked up to the boat, the ride is really great! And serving Jesus can be just as fun and exciting!

PRAYER:

God, may our lives show that we believe in you, and are ready to serve. Amen.

SUMMER

LICK IT! SLURP IT!

THEME: Worship from the heart

OBJECT: Ice cream in a cone

TEXT: The time is coming when the true worshipers will worship the Father in spirit and truth. That time is now here. And these are the kinds of worshipers the Father wants. God is spirit. Those who worship God must worship in spirit and truth. *John 4:23, 24*

APPLICATION:

Who likes ice cream? Nothing tastes as great on a hot summer day as an ice cream cone. There are many flavors, and lots of ways to eat an ice cream cone! I like to lick around the edges first *(demonstrate),* so the ice cream doesn't melt and run down the sides. Some would rather lick up one side and down the other, or you may like to just slurp it from the top. I have a friend who makes a lot more noise eating than I do! Some people eat slow, and some eat fast. Some eat the ice cream, and then the cone, some eat them both together. There are those who like to eat outside in the hot sun, and those who eat inside so the ice cream doesn't melt as quickly.

Are there wrong ways to eat ice cream? No, just favorite ways. However you eat your cone, it is important to get it eaten before the ice cream runs down your arm and drips off your elbow. That really makes a mess!

Just as there are many good ways to eat an ice cream cone, our church service includes a lot of good ways to worship God. What are some of the ways we worship? *(Discuss singing, praying, reading the Bible, etc.)* Do you have a way you especially like? *(Discuss.)* You can tell that we don't all have the same favorite way to praise the Lord. Some people like to sing first, and then pray. Others would rather have a message before the offering is taken. Many like slow songs, others like to sing fast. We all have favorite ways to worship Jesus. Different ways are not wrong—they are just different! We can waste so much time deciding what way to worship that we don't have time to enjoy worshiping. The important thing is that we love Jesus with all our hearts, and tell him so when we worship.

PRAYER:

Lord, no matter how many different ways we worship you, may we always worship with love and praise coming right from our hearts! Amen.

SUMMER

UGLY BAIT

THEME: Watch out for sin; avoid temptation.

OBJECTS: Various fishing lures

TEXT: Test everything. Keep what is good. And stay away from everything that is evil. *1 Thessalonians 5: 21, 22*

APPLICATION:

Has anyone here ever gone fishing? *(Responses.)* What did you use to catch the fish? *(Responses.)* It is always interesting to see the different things fishermen use to catch fish. It would seem that no self-respecting fish could be caught by the likes of some of these lures. Look at what I've brought along. Here's a really bright one. Does this look like something to eat? Of course not. I can show you this one that makes noise to attract the fish (*rattle*), or this one that even glows in the dark, for the fish wanting a late night snack. You can even buy smelly stuff to spray on the bait to make the fish want to bite. And the live bait already smells pretty awful!

You wouldn't think a smart fish would go for these lures, would you—but they do. The fish doesn't find out how wrong he was until after he's hooked! Sin can attract us like that. It gets our attention by looking like something really good. We find ourselves wanting something very much even if we know it's sinful or wrong. Perhaps you found some money left around the house that you thought no one would miss. Or maybe you saw a candy bar on a store shelf, but you didn't have enough money to buy it. Did you think "Who would miss just one candy bar?" You wouldn't think smart people would be attracted to sin, but we are. When you're tempted to do something you know is wrong, just remember the fish that lost its life for the love of an ugly lure. Don't think you won't get hooked. Even small sins can get us into trouble, and giving in to small temptations leads us to even bigger trouble! The Bible reminds us to test everything (that means think about what you're about to do). Keep doing what is good. And stay away from everything that is evil. Let's ask God to help us to make good choices—and stay away from sin, especially when we're tempted to do things we know are wrong.

PRAYER:

Lord, help us when we are tempted. We want to avoid evil, and live for you. Amen.

SUMMER

A FLY'S LiFE

THEME: God's gift to us: eternal life

OBJECT: Fly swatter

TEXT: For God loved the world so much that he gave his only Son. God gave his Son so that whoever believes in him may not be lost, but have eternal life. *John 3:16*

APPLICATION:

This time of the year, bugs really bug me. There are places you can't sit down without being joined by a whole bunch of pesky flies. If you don't want to use a smelly candle to keep them away, the only thing you can do is use a fly swatter. A buzzing fly can be a real pain. And using a fly swatter is a useful solution—unless you're a fly. Did you ever think about that? Imagine settling down to pizza, and having a huge fly swatter come down on you. Imagine playing with your friends, and swish, you're flipped across the room. Imagine taking a nap on a hymnbook and smack, the book closes on you. For a fly, that is the end of its life.

Fortunately, we aren't flies. God made a way for us to have eternal life. We can try to avoid danger. We can take care of the bodies God has given us. We can keep clean, eat healthy foods, and be careful when we cross the street, but these are not the things that make it possible for us to live forever. We can live forever only because Jesus came and died on the cross to take our sins away. And if we accept him into our hearts, he promises to give us eternal life.

Having Jesus in our hearts makes us different from flies that can be wiped out forever. Our bodies will die someday, but our spirits will live forever. Christians have no reason to fear because we know Jesus, and someday we will live with him forever in Heaven.

PRAYER:

Thank you, God, for a life without fear, because we belong to you. Amen.

SUMMER

GO ONE WAY

THEME: Unity

OBJECTS: Water skis, a towrope, a helper if you wish

TEXT: Does your life in Christ give you strength? Does his love comfort you? Do we share together in the Spirit? Do you have mercy and kindness? If so, make me very happy by having the same thoughts, sharing the same love, and having one mind and purpose.　　　　　*Philippians 2:1, 2*

APPLICATION:

Few things are as much fun as waterskiing. After you put the skis on your feet, you sit in the water and wait as the boat gets lined up. *(Have helper sit on a ledge with skis on, and hang on to the handle at the end of the rope.)* Then, when you are ready, you hang onto the rope, really, really tight, and yell "hit it!" The boat pulling you puts it in high gear, and you're pulled to your feet—hopefully. Sometimes you can't get up because one foot goes left and the other foot goes right. That's really embarrassing, especially if you swallow a lot of water, or others see your spectacular fall. When you are learning to ski, you fall more than you ski because it takes a lot of practice to get the skis to go in the same direction.

Sometimes we have the same problem with our friends. We may get along just fine one day, and look forward to more good times. But the next day we may want to do one thing and our friend may want to do something very different. We can't always think exactly the same. Each of us has different needs and different things we want to do.

As Christians we need to think of ourselves as joined together—just as firmly as if we were one pair of skis on two legs. We are all part of the body of Christ—and since we are brought together by him, we need to work together with one Spirit and purpose. When we fall—or don't get along—we need to get up, keep on trying to love each other, and continue serving God together. We ski best, and serve God best, when we are going in the same direction.

PRAYER:

Dear God, help us always to remember that as Christians we are joined together, and we need to work together in love. Amen.

42

AUTUMN

ERASED

THEME: Forgiven sin

OBJECTS: A No. 2 pencil with an eraser, a pad of paper

TEXT: If we confess our sins, he will forgive our sins. We can trust God. He does what is right. He will make us clean from all the wrongs we have done.
1 John 1:9

APPLICATION:

Some people like to write with pens, but I like using a pencil. This is a brand new pencil, and if you look carefully, you can see "No. 2" written across the side. "No. 2" on a pencil means the lead is a little soft.

I just sharpened my pencil, and you can see how well it writes. *(Demonstrate by writing the word "sin" as "zin." For young children, just draw a line.)* Sometimes, even when I try hard, I make mistakes. I'm happy that the pencil has an eraser, and that the mistake I've made can be taken away. *(Erase the "z" and correct it, or erase the line.)*

We are like this pencil. Even though we may try hard to do everything right, we make mistakes. We can't take away sin ourselves. We need to tell Jesus that we are sorry, and give him first place in our lives. He is the only one who can erase the wrong things we have done. *(Erase the word "sin.")* He forgives and gives us a clean start. With him in our lives, we can learn from our mistakes.

PRAYER:

Dear God, may we know and remind each other that our sins can be erased through Jesus Christ, our Savior. Amen.

FiLLED UP

THEME: Being filled with good things

OBJECTS: Backpack filled with articles—some beautiful and useful, some old and useless

TEXT: A good person has good things saved up in his heart. And so he brings good things out of his heart. But an evil person has evil things saved up in his heart. So he brings out bad things. A person speaks the things that are in his heart. *Luke 6:45*

APPLiCATioN:

Do you ever carry your things in a backpack? I'm wearing mine today. Let's see what's in here. *(Take off and empty.)* A beautiful banana, a Bible, a rotten apple, an old dirty sock, and some trash. You see, I put some good things in my pack, and I also put in some junk. When I put good things in, then good things come out. When I put bad things in, bad things come out. It's as simple as that!

Our lives can also be filled with either good or bad things. We can spend our time reading our Bible, or we can spend our time watching TV. We can spend time talking with Jesus, or we can spend our time talking to our friends, saying things that are unkind about others. We can say helpful words to each other, or we can fill our mouths with nasty comments that hurt. A good way to fill up with good is to spend time thinking about things that are good—things that are worthy of praise, true, honorable, right, pure and beautiful and respected (Philippians 4:8). Only when we are filled with good things will good things come out. Our words will then be helpful and kind.

PRAYER:

Lord God, help us to fill our hearts with good, so that we can share that good with others. Amen.

AUTUMN
UNIQUE GiFTS

THEME: All our talents are precious to God.

OBJECTS: Colored leaves

TEXT: God has given each of us the ability to do certain things well.
Romans 12:6, TLB

APPLICATiON:

The trees are especially pretty this time of the year, aren't they? What makes them so beautiful? *(Discuss changing colors.)* Do any of you have a favorite color? *(Discuss.)* If you like red best, would the trees be prettier if all leaves were red? If your favorite color is yellow, would autumn be better if all leaves were yellow? *(No.)*

What makes autumn special is that there are many different colors and shapes of leaves on the trees. Just like leaves are different from each other, God made each of us different from each other. Not only are we different colors and shapes, we are also good at doing different things. While I may think my talent is best, and you may think yours is best, the truth is that it is the combination of all of our talents that makes our church able to do so much. What if all of us were singers, but no one knew how to teach? What if everyone could teach, but no one could make pretty bulletin boards? Who can tell me some other things people do at church to help? *(With each job, describe some talent needed.)* We can get every job done, because we are all different and all have our own unique talents.

PRAYER:

We praise you, Lord, for giving each of us something we can do well. Help us to use our talents for you. Amen.

DON'T WIPE OUT!

THEME: Forgiving each other

OBJECTS: Downhill skis and boots

TEXT: Do not be angry with each other, but forgive each other If someone does wrong to you, then forgive him. Forgive each other because the Lord forgave you. Do all these things; but most important, love each other. Love is what holds you all together in perfect unity.

Colossians 3:13, 14

APPLICATION:

These are downhill skis. See how the boots are locked onto the skis? You can move them quickly from side to side *(hold the skis parallel and demonstrate, point-ing tips from side to side)* as you glide safely to the bottom of the hill. That's how it is supposed to go, but that's not what always happens. Too often the right ski goes left, and the left ski goes right *(demonstrate)*. What happens when they cross? Yes, major wipeout! Nothing more happens until the skier digs himself out of the snow, and gets the skis working together again.

Just as skis don't always go the same direction, we don't always go in the same direction as other people. You may be determined to play a game, but your friend wants to watch television. You may want to eat pizza but your mother has prepared roast beef. Or maybe you and your friend want to play with the same toy at the same time. What happens when you and others don't have the same idea? *(Discuss the possibility of fighting, or a wipeout of the friendship.)*

Even in our church we may not always agree. In fact, sometimes our disagree-ments lead to arguments and angry feelings. The Bible tells us that instead of always wanting our own way we must be tied together in love. And when we do disagree or hurt each other, God wants us to forgive—and not stay angry. Like a skier who comes to a fast stop when skis cross, nothing good happens if we are constantly crossing each other because we insist on having our own way all of the time. God's love in our hearts should help us work together just as two skis working together can glide smoothly down the hill. Jesus was always concerned with what others wanted and needed. Let's follow his example of love and for-giveness!

PRAYER:

Lord, help us to not always insist on having our own way, but to be like Jesus, working together and forgiving each other when we disagree. Amen.

WARMED BY GOD'S LOVE

THEME: Fellowship

OBJECTS: A mitten and a glove

TEXT: Do not be interested only in your own life, but be interested in the lives of others. In your lives you must think and act like Christ Jesus.

Philippians 2:4, 5

APPLICATION:

Some people say that if you have cold hands you have a warm heart, but when my hands are cold, I'm cold all over.

When it's cold outside, it's important to keep your hands warm. What are some ways we can do that? *(Responses.)* We could keep our hands in our pockets all the time. That would keep our hands warm, but it would prevent us from doing anything else with our hands. We could also wear gloves or mittens. Gloves look great. *(Put on a glove.)* Each finger gets wrapped up in its own little space, and stays much warmer than it would outside of the glove. But when I wear gloves, I sometimes have to pull all of my fingers back inside the palm part to get them warm. *(Demonstrate.)* Some people don't like the way mittens look. *(Put on a mitten.)* They think it's more grown up to wear gloves. Still, even they must admit that when all their fingers are close together in a mitten, they stay much warmer. On the coldest of days, I think mittens are the best choice!

The Bible tells us that we are supposed to care about and look out for others just as we look out for ourselves. Too often, like each finger in a glove, we stay apart from others and think only about ourselves. It's easy to get busy with our own needs and wants and forget about a friend who may need our help. Jesus taught us to help others. He knows how important it is to be close to and care for each other. Just as our fingers keep each other warm in a mitten, so caring about each other brings the warmth of God's love to our lives. It's always more fun walking to school with someone than walking alone. Many jobs can be finished faster and be fun with the help of a friend. So let's be like fingers in a mitten instead of a glove. Let's be interested in, and care about, each other, so the love of God will warm our hearts and lives.

PRAYER:

Jesus, help us to not only think of our own needs, but also the needs of others. Amen.

MELT NOT

THEME: Jesus never changes.

OBJECTS: Snowballs, tape of the song "Frosty the Snowman," cassette player

TEXT: Jesus Christ is the same yesterday, today, and forever.

Hebrews 13:8

APPLICATION:

Turn on the radio around Christmastime, and you will hear this song about "Frosty the Snowman." *(Play the song as the children listen.)* Many people make snowmen, depending of course on where they live. Do you remember how Frosty was made? Children rolled big snowballs, much larger than I brought along today. Then they stacked the snowballs. *(Demonstrate.)* What else did they put on Frosty? He was very handsome with his "button nose and two eyes made out of coal." But the story has a sad ending. What happened when the children came out to play with Frosty? Yes, he had melted in the warm sun, and only bits of coal, the button, and his clothes remained. The kids couldn't count on him to play then, could they?

The opposite is true about Jesus. While the kids couldn't depend on Frosty staying around to play—especially when summer rolled around—the Bible promises that Jesus will always be there for us. He won't disappear, no matter what the weather. He remains right beside us all the time. We can depend on Jesus no matter where we are or what happens in our lives.

PRAYER:

God, we thank you that we can trust you to be with us always. Amen.